How to Draw a Dinosaur

T0321564

Contents

Written by Rob Alcraft

Illustrated by James Cottell

Collins

Dare to draw a dinosaur!

Come on a dinosaur drawing adventure. Learn simple tricks to draw these prehistoric giants.

Learn to draw Tyrannosaurus

Meet Tyrannosaurus. It was a gigantic killer that hunted other dinosaurs.

This is a Tyrannosaurus thigh bone!

1 Sketch a half circle.

body

Use a pencil – swap to working in pen later.

2 Add a rectangle.

head

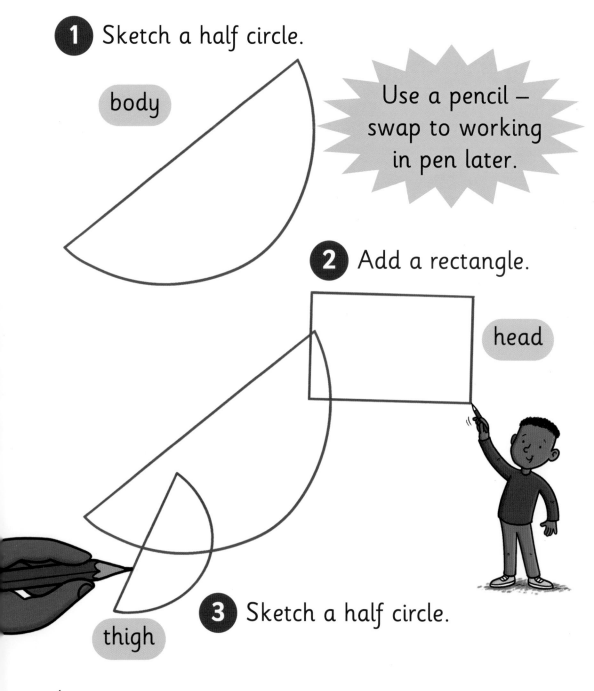

3 Sketch a half circle.

thigh

4 Add a rectangle.

5 Add a half circle.

foot

Tyrannosaurus teeth could crunch through gristle, muscle and bone.

6 Add another matching leg.

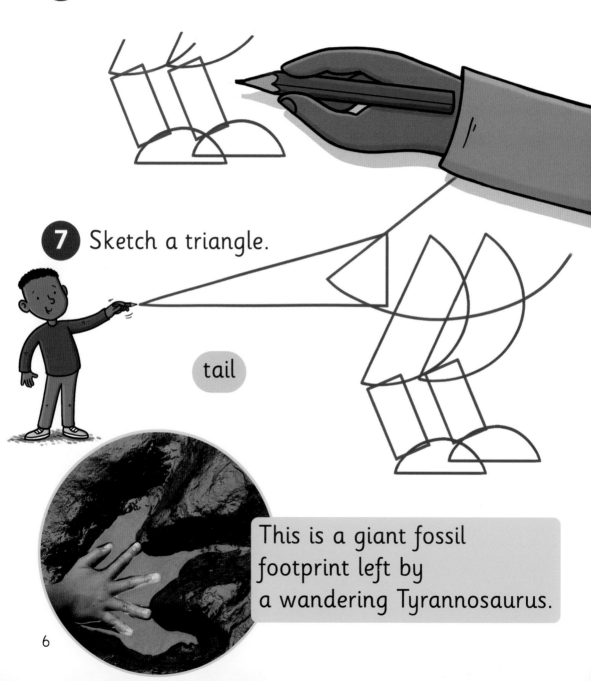

7 Sketch a triangle.

tail

This is a giant fossil footprint left by a wandering Tyrannosaurus.

8 Use rectangles for arms.

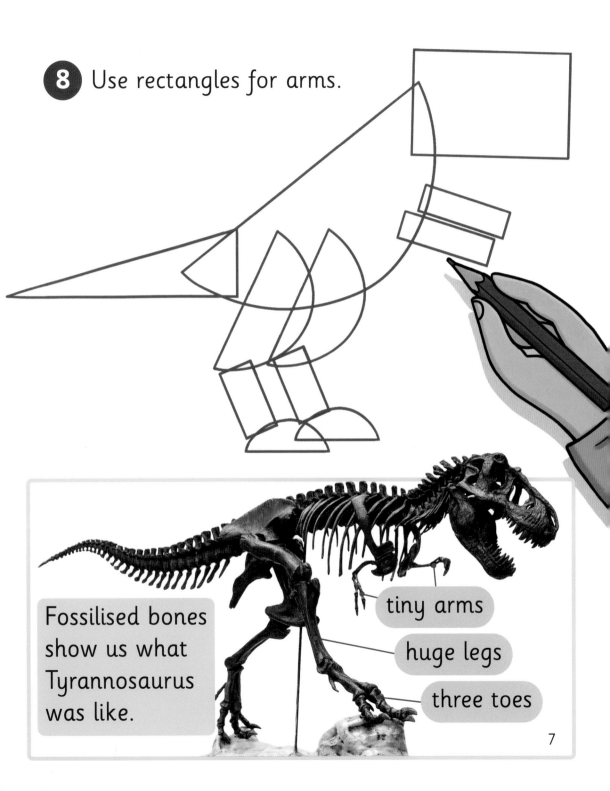

tiny arms

huge legs

three toes

Fossilised bones show us what Tyrannosaurus was like.

9 Work up your sketch in pen.

Watch out!
Tyrannosaurus had
enormous teeth.
Here's one at actual size!

10 Now sketch a face and features.

What kind of character could you give your dinosaur? Try different curves and eye shapes.

goofy

angry

scared

calm

11 What will your Tyrannosaurus look like?

Think colour!
Research on fossil dinosaur bones shows that some could have been covered in very vivid markings.

Learn to draw Triceratops

Meet Triceratops. This immense plant-eating creature walked the earth at the same time as Tyrannosaurus.

Triceratops had a huge head!

1 Sketch a big egg-shape.

2 Add a half circle.

3 Add a rectangle.

head

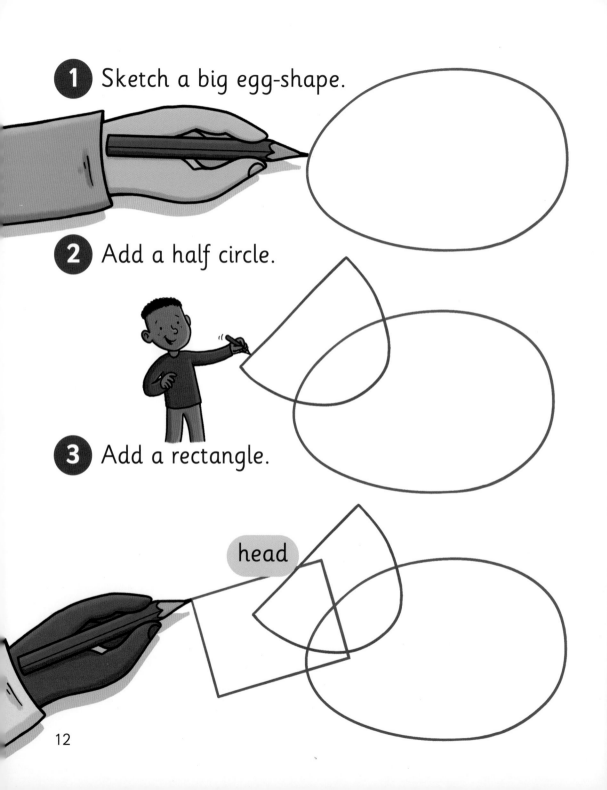

4 Half circles work for thighs.

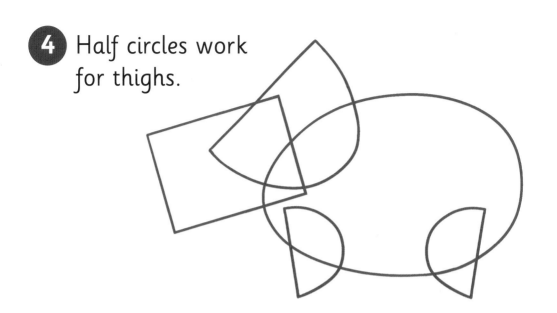

5 Use rectangles for lower legs.

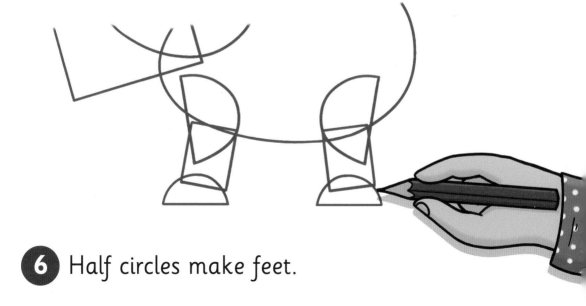

6 Half circles make feet.

Triceratops was enormous — the same size as a lorry!

"Triceratops" means "three-horned face"!

7 Now add the matching legs.

8 Sketch a triangle.

tail

This is a fossilised baby dinosaur in its egg. Even huge Triceratops grew from small eggs like these.

9 Sketch three spiky horns.

10 Draw a beak.

11 Add an eye.

12 Notice these toes.

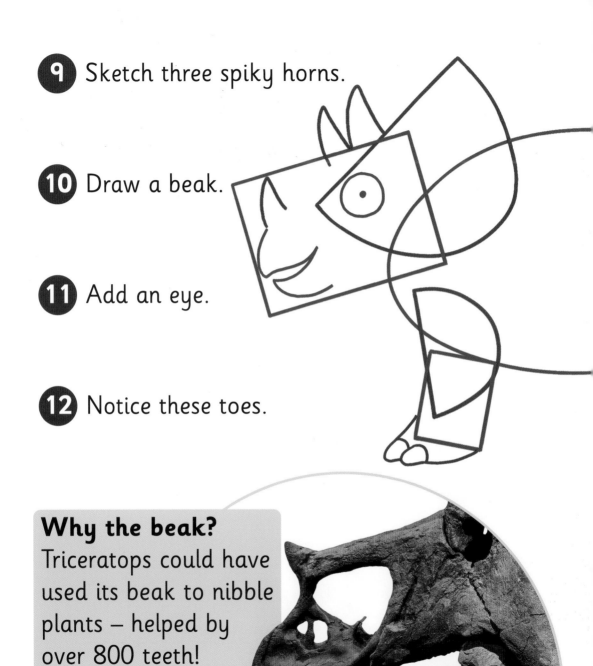

Why the beak?
Triceratops could have used its beak to nibble plants – helped by over 800 teeth!

13 Work with a pen to finish your picture.

Some dinosaur scientists think Triceratops might have had colourful markings – like this lizard.

Now, what character could you give your Triceratops?

grumpy

terrified

blissful

talkative

14 Triceratops is ready. Which markings will you choose?

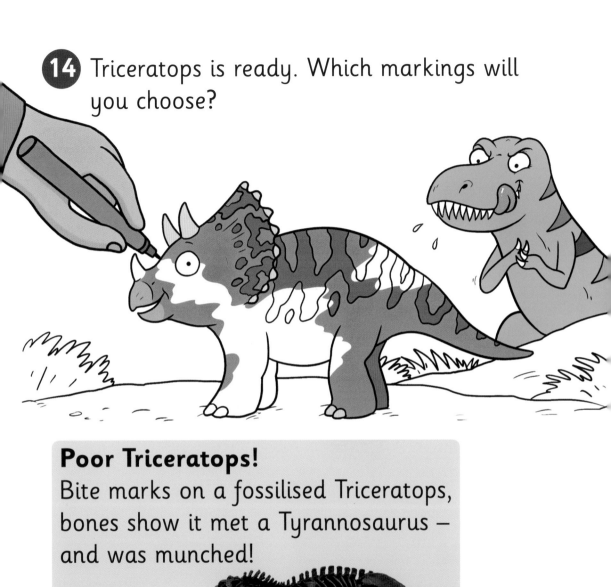

Poor Triceratops!
Bite marks on a fossilised Triceratops, bones show it met a Tyrannosaurus – and was munched!

Triceratops meets Tyrannosaurus

Now you can complete your dinosaur picture. What about adding the ooze and mud of a swamp?

What should go where?

Can you match each fossil
with its dinosaur owner?

Review: After reading

Use your assessment from hearing the children read to choose any GPCs, words or tricky words that need additional practice.

Read 1: Decoding

- Ask the children to read the following words. Can they identify the different sounds made by the digraph 'al' and the grapheme 'a'?
  - **small** (/or/)
  - **half** (/ar/)
  - **calm** (/ar/)
  - **walked** (/or/)
  - **talkative** (/or/)
- Challenge the children to take turns to read an instruction (1 to 6) on pages 12 and 13. Say: Can you blend in your head when you read the words?

Read 2: Prosody

- Turn to pages 8 and 9.
- Discuss why a reader might emphasise **Now** at the beginning of page 9. (e.g. *it emphasises that this is the next stage*)
- Encourage the children to emphasise the pronoun **your** in the question on page 9. Ask: What effect does the emphasis have? (e.g. *focusing the attention on each reader's own sketch*)
- Let the children experiment with emphasising different words on page 9, to clarify the meaning.

Read 3: Comprehension

- Ask the children what they knew already about the dinosaurs mentioned in this book, and the features of each. Where did they get the information?
- Ask the children what sort of book this is. (*an instruction book*)
  - Ask: What features make it an instruction book? (e.g. *numbered points, command words, diagrams*)
  - Ask: Are there any bits of text that aren't instructions? (*the fact boxes*)
- Turn to page 9 and point to the word **features**. Encourage the children to come up with a definition of what is meant by this in the context of drawing a dinosaur face. (e.g. *the face parts that make the dinosaur look different, such as raised brows, smiling mouth*)
- Hold a quiz and ask the children to skim and scan the pages for answers. For example, ask:
  - Which dinosaur has 800 teeth? (*Triceratops, page 16*)
  - What are the two stages of drawing a dinosaur? (e.g. *sketching it using shapes; adding the features*)
- Look together at pages 22 and 23. Can the children identify the fossils that belong to each dinosaur?